Simple Solutions™
Clicker Training

By
Arden Moore
Illustrations by Buck Jones

Plus Training Tips

NUDGE

CLICK

BOWTIE
P R E S S®

A Division of BowTie, Inc.
Irvine, California

D1535690

Karla Austin, *Business Operations Manager*
Nick Clemente, *Special Consultant*
Jarelle S. Stein, *Editor*
Jennifer Perumean, *Assistant Editor*
Jill Dupont, *Production*
Michael Vincent Capozzi, *Book Designer*

The dogs in this book are referred to as *he* and *she* in alternating chapters.

Library of Congress Cataloging-in-Publication Data

Moore, Arden.
  Clicker training / by Arden Moore ; illustrations by Buck Jones.
    p. cm. -- (Simple solutions)
  ISBN 1-931993-58-0
  1. Dogs--Training. 2. Clicker training (Animal training) I. Title. II. Series: Simple solutions (Irvine, Calif.)

  SF431.M8145 2005
  636.7'0887--dc22
                                        2004024832

BowTie Press®
A Division of BowTie, Inc.
3 Burroughs
Irvine, California 92618

Printed and bound in Singapore
10 9 8 7 6 5 4 3 2 1

Contents

Introduction

The headliner at SeaWorld weighs a mighty seven tons and answers to "Shamu." People from all over come to the San Diego theme park to witness this killer whale soar high in the air on cue and create a mega splash that soaks the first fifteen rows.

At county fairs, clever chickens peck the appropriate lever to win a food prize. In some indoor arenas, smart cats soar over hurdles and race up ramps to win blue ribbons. Why mention these feats in a dog book? Because Shamu, chickens, and cats have a lot in common with some talented canines: all learned their tricks through clicker training.

This positive technique relies on operant conditioning to shape a desired behavior without force or cajoling. The premise is simple: performing appropriate actions and behaviors earns rewards. The notion of operant conditioning first gained prominence in the 1920s, when Harvard psychologists B. F. Skinner and Fred Keller successfully shaped human behaviors in positive ways. Keller and Marian Breland expanded this concept to the animal world in the 1940s, amazing crowds with raccoons, parrots, and sheep trained to perform tricks at the sound of a whistle.

About two decades ago, veteran dolphin trainer Karen Pryor began experimenting with dog training. She traded her whistle for a clicker. In no time, she was curing doggie misdeeds, introducing welcomed actions, and sharing her expertise with people worldwide.

In this book, you will learn how the clicker technique serves as a universal language for communication between people and their dogs and discover the countless ways you can put clicker training to use.

Well-timed clicks aid in basic obedience training, reshape canine negative personalities, make grooming sessions less stressful, stop unwanted behaviors, hone agility skills, and teach advanced tricks. Clicker training gives your dog the chance to learn how to learn and teaches him it's okay to make choices.

Grab a clicker, call your dog, and let's get started!

Get Ready—Clickers, Locales, Treats, and Timing

Setting up for success begins with laying a solid foundation before launching into clicker training. First, you need a sound maker. The most common device is an inexpensive metal clicker found at pet supply stores. Depress the metal flap to create the distinctive, crisp sound. You can also make a clicking sound with a ballpoint pen or with your tongue. Whatever tool you pick, stick with it so your dog knows *that* sound signals the start of a fun learning session.

Next, select a good place and time for tutoring your dog. Train in a quiet room without distractions. Turn off the television and usher the cat out. Choose a time for learning when you're not stressed.

Motivate your pooch by offering her premium treats, such as roasted chicken or diced cheese. Tasty, soft people food will get her moving faster than hard kibble. Treats should be no bigger than a pea; just enough for her to quickly bite and swallow while remaining focused on training.

Train between meals. Your dog may be more apt to work for treats if you pick up her food bowls a couple hours before you begin. To prevent weight gain in chubby dogs, reduce daily food amounts by about 10 percent.

In clicker training, timing is paramount. Depress the clicker the instant your dog performs each step of the desired behavior, then treat. Don't wait until she completes a multi-step trick. Delays can confuse your canine student.

Keep your clicker with you inside the home so you can click cute antics and actions, such as bowing or raising a front paw. Strategically place clickers in rooms your dog frequents. If you're having problems getting to a clicker in time, keep one in your pocket.

Build on small successes by keeping practice sessions short—less than three minutes—to decrease risk of boring or overtaxing your dog. Never force her into a movement. Instead, coax her with the sound of the click followed by treats or praise. In a multi-pet household, hold individual training sessions. Build confidence by testing your clicker technique on the dog most curious and willing to learn.

Be patient. If you're feeling frustrated, try again later. Your dog can read your mood. Remind yourself that this training should bring out the best in your dog and strengthen your bond.

Make Training a Snap— Doggy Basics

Learning the basics can be just a click away—whether your student is a puppy, an adult dog needing a refresher course, or a newly adopted dog. Your dog will comply with your requests because he views you as a fun teacher and leader.

Turn the all-important *come* command into a fun game. Duck into a closet or a room out of your dog's sight. Say his name and the word, "come." The instant he comes to

you, click and treat him. Select different places (not too hidden). Ask a family member or a friend to join the come-find-me game. Stop the game while your dog is still interested; don't wait until he grows bored. Above all, make sure

your dog receives a treat for finding you.

Never use the clicker itself to call your dog; it may confuse him into thinking the clicker is a cue for the *come* command. This will weaken the clicker's purpose of reinforcing a variety of behaviors. Never issue the *come* command and click if you are going to reprimand your dog for a misdeed. Associating the click and *come* with punishment, he will be less apt to obey.

If you are annoyed by a dog who yelps and hovers underfoot as you prepare his meal, then designate an out-of-the-way place for him to wait. At dinnertime, prepare your dog's dish, set it aside, and bring out premium treats. Select a doggie bed or rug situated so he can easily see the actions in the kitchen. Use a target or a bit of food to encourage him to sit on his bed or rug. As soon as he does, click and treat. If he stays on the spot for five seconds or so, click and treat again.

Don't speak during this mini training session. Click and treat your dog for staying on the spot, varying the time between three and fifteen seconds. Then click and set his food bowl on the floor.

Repeat these steps the next day, but increase his waiting time by touching the counter and opening the refrigerator while he is on the spot. You are saying: stay on the spot to get clicked, even if I'm doing something else in the

kitchen. If he leaves his spot, lure him back and then click

and treat. In time, your dog will learn that by sitting still on

the spot, he will be rewarded with his meal.

Introducing a crate for those times when you need to safely confine your dog because you can't supervise him is easy with the clicker technique. First, leave the door open to let your dog explore the crate freely. Click and treat when he looks at the crate, when he steps toward it, when he sniffs it, and when he puts his head through the doorway. Next, toss a treat inside. Give verbal kudos when he enters to eat the treat; do not praise him when he exits. Toss a toy inside, and click when he enters to play with it. Introduce a cue word or phrase such as "crate is great" as you toss in a treat.

With your dog inside the crate, offer him small treats and plenty of praise. Stop when he exits. Then toss a treat or a toy inside and shut the door once he reenters. Walk away, returning to him only when he is quiet.

Repeat these steps, building up the time your dog spends inside the crate. When he can remain for at least thirty minutes, he is ready to sleep in it. At bedtime, move the crate to your bedroom so he won't feel isolated and you can hear him if he needs to go out.

A dog is a den animal and must learn his crate is a positive place. Never use it for punishment.

Click Away Destructive Chewing and Digging

Many dogs seem to be programmed with "got-to-dig" software and demonstrate this on your garden or even your living room carpet. Use clicker training to redirect dogs toward appropriate digging areas.

Start in your backyard. First, make the No Dog Zones less appealing and less accessible. Spray citrus or other dog-repelling scents around the outside of your garden bed, and install fencing difficult to climb over. Next, find a

small space you can designate as a doggy digging center. Fill an area at least four by four feet with sand and border it with low-level fencing.

While your dog watches, bury some biscuits and favorite toys in the sand. Call her over to her sand pile. When she starts to dig, click and treat and offer praise. If she heads to your garden or another wrong place, redirect her to her digging area and click and treat.

To tame a chew-happy nature, you must first recognize that all dogs chew to some degree. Inappropriate chewing often results from boredom or anxiety. Your dog may not be getting enough physical stimulation, may need longer walks or time at a doggie day care center to unleash pent-up energy.

Rely on these clicker tactics to save your possessions from becoming chew toys.

- Patrol your house and make sure potential chew objects are stored out of your dog's reach.
- Confine your dog to safe areas of the house with gates or other barriers when you're not around.
- Spray bitter or another dog repellant on inappropriate chew objects to make them less appealing. Boil a

Nylabone in chicken broth to make it more appealing.

• Teach her the *leave it* command. Place a shoe and a chew toy in front of her and encourage her with a clicker and food treat to chew the toy rather than the shoe.

• Redirect your dog away from the shoe by making a noise such as "aaaack" and guiding her to the chew toy. Click and treat so she learns she gets doubly rewarded with a toy and a treat when she chews on appropriate objects.

The key is patience and consistency. Always immediately follow a click with a treat during training time.

Click the Bite
Out of Nipping

Love to cuddle your puppy until—ouch!—his needle-sharp teeth sink into your hand? Puppies taken from a litter too young may not have learned bite inhibition from their mothers and littermates.

To turn painful nips into welcomed kisses, remember the advice:

• Never permit your puppy to play with your hands or clothes. Do this by stopping playtime and leaving.

- Act like a statue the second your puppy grabs you or your clothing to take the fun out of the nip.
- Provide an appropriate chew toy, such as knotted rope or sockcovered tennis ball, when he starts to nip.

To clicker train nips away begin by clos-ing your fist and placing it in front of your pup's face. Click and treat if he doesn't nip. Repeat. If he only bumps his soft nose against your fist, that's great—click this! Wave your closed fist slowly around in front

of your puppy and click and treat each time he does not try to nip. Repeat several times. Work on increasing the time and altering the distance and speed of your fist. Click each time he doesn't nip and treat. Repeat these steps while substituting a toy or bone for your closed fist. Click and treat for calmness and for not grabbing at the object. If he tries to nip, stop; move the object out of sight and start again a little farther away.

When you have clicked and treated him several times for staying calm, click and give him the object to enjoy. Now, you're ready to follow these steps with your open hand,

shirtsleeve, and index finger to help your puppy learn not to nip objects near his face.

To stop unwanted nipping, you must also teach your puppy the *close your mouth* command. Stand up and take your hands away when he shows signs of nipping. Watch closely. The second he closes his mouth, give the *close your mouth* command, click, and treat. Repeat.

The final, but very important, tip: teach other family members these steps to ensure consistent training.

Silence! Tone Down Barking

The doorbell rings and your dog unleashes a series of ear-piercing yips or floor-shaking woofs. Shouting at her only escalates the volume. Fortunately, clicker training will silence this noisy nuisance.

To retrain your dog, make sure you have a clicker and a big bowl of highly desirable small treats. Call your dog to the front door and stand close to her. Knock on the door (or have a friend knock or ring the doorbell). When your

dog barks once, click and treat. As she eats the treat, put your hand in front of her face like a policeman signaling traffic to stop. Do not touch her face. When she stops or backs up a bit, click.

The idea is to generate the first bark, click and treat, then put out your hand stop sign and click and treat when she backs up a bit and is quiet. Your dog will soon learn that she gets paid for limited barking and paid when she stops barking. This way, your dog still gets to be protective, but no longer engages in excessive barking.

Curb Leash Yanking

Even a twelve-pound dachshund can turn into a mass of pulling muscle if he spots a squirrel he must chase, suddenly turning your relaxed walk into a tug-of-war.

The conventional wisdom among dog trainers teaches people to act like trees the moment their dogs begin to pull or to turn and walk the other way. That may work for some dogs, but for those it doesn't, clicker training can put the brakes on leash pulling.

First, put the leash on your dog and stand motionless.

The second he releases tension on the leash, click and show him a treat you have in your hand. Let him see you place the treat on the ground by the outside of your left foot. Once he's eaten the treat, move so the leash is taut and stand quietly. Click when he moves to release the tension. Show him the treat and place it by your left foot. Repeat several times.

Next, stand and click for eye contact. After the click, place a treat by your left foot. After your dog has finished eating the treat, remember to move to the end of the leash. Click and treat three times for looking at you while on a loose leash. Stand by your dog. Making sure he is eyeing you, toss treats right past his nose to about three feet away. When he eats the treats and comes back to you looking for more, click and treat by placing the food by the outside of your left foot. Move and repeat.

Again, toss the treat past your dog's nose. When he finishes eating and turns to come back, turn and start walking (just a few steps at first). When he catches up, just reaching your pant leg, click and treat. Repeat.

These four steps serve as a foundation. Let's move into advance training—for those times you want to curtail

leash pulling due to distractions, such as the approach of

another dog outdoors. First, communicate some calming

signals to your dog to let him know the approaching dog

does not bother you. Loosen the leash and turn your head, lick your lips, move sideways, or yawn. Stop, stretch and give your dog a friendly head scratch to get him into a relaxed mood.

Note at what point your dog freezes, holds his ears erect, and delivers a steadfast stare at the approaching dog. Does he do so at 50 feet or 100 feet away? Find the point so that you can begin desensitization a few feet before your dog displays this behavior.

Your goal is to prevent activation of the trigger, to catch your dog doing something good, and to reinforce that

behavior. To do so, keep your pocket full of strongly scented, tasty, tiny snacks such as Pounce cat treats—perfect training treats for dogs. Chicken cooked in garlic works well, too.

When the other dog nears the point at which your pooch begins to display inappropriate reactions, turn slightly into your dog so he has to look up at you to avoid being stepped on. Click, say a crisp "yes," and give him a treat for his attention. Move toward him another step, say "yes" or click, and give another treat. Keep moving him in a circular manner away from the other dog.

Turn your back to the oncoming dog and reward your pooch for keeping his attention on you. Use your happiest voice while madly clicking and treating. Throw off calming signals such as yawning. If your dog still fixates on the stranger, continue turning circles with him so his focus switches to you. The other animal will probably pass the two of you without giving your dog time to stress. Continue practicing in places where he will encounter other dogs on leash.

The more you reinforce calm behavior, the sooner he will come to realize there is nothing to fear and no reason to challenge other dogs. He can look to you for leadership and for all good things.

Good Dogs Don't Jump

Dogs naturally leap up and lick other dogs as a form of canine greeting. However, some jump-happy hounds can literally knock people over with their desire for affection and attention. To convert your jumper into a well-mannered greeter, introduce clicker training, heeding these tips:

- Never pet, praise, or give any attention to your dog while she is jumping.
- *Do* pet, praise, and give positive attention when your dog has all four paws touching the floor.

- Alert family members and houseguests to be consistent in discouraging jumping.

To begin the lessons, take some treats and a clicker outside. Ring the bell and enter the front door. Immediately bend over while your dog still has all her feet on the ground and click. At the same time, push a small treat against her nose and then drop it so she must bend to eat it.

Repeat this action until your dog starts standing and waiting, perhaps even looking at the floor when you enter. Then have a family member or friend repeat the steps.

Here's another clicker option. Enter the front door, fold your arms, give the *sit* command, and click and treat. This body posture is less inviting to a jump-happy dog.

Cool Clicker Tricks

Not every dog will master every clicker-induced trick. Your dog's repertoire depends on his motivation level and your imagination and patience level. You can wow friends by teaching your dog fun and functional tricks such as flipping light switches, retrieving TV remotes, and balancing biscuits on his nose. The real trick to such training comes in successfully linking a sequence of mini steps.

Let's illustrate with the art of balancing a biscuit on the muzzle. Start your dog in a sitting position. Click and give

a treat. Be sure you have your dog's attention. Lightly place your left hand under his chin to position his muzzle so it's parallel to the floor for a steady surface. Initially cup your hand under your dog's chin for a couple seconds, then click and treat with your right hand.

Next sequence: hold the biscuit on your dog's muzzle for a second or two. Then click and treat. As he seems to let the biscuit stay on his nose, increase the time by a few seconds before clicking and treating.

Once your dog shows he will leave the biscuit on his nose without shaking it off, slowly move your hand away.

Click and treat by removing the biscuit from his muzzle and handing it to him.

Final stage: get your dog to keep the biscuit balanced on his muzzle for a few seconds without your hand cupping his chin. Click and treat. You're now ready to introduce the final step—getting your dog to toss the biscuit into the air and catch it before it hits the floor. Do this by issuing a command such as *grab it* as you knock the treat off his muzzle to the side, making sure you catch it in your hand and deliver it to your dog. This is a good way to communicate your intentions. Slowly encourage the grab-

the-treat behavior by clicking your dog as soon as he catches the biscuit in the air.

Be patient with your dog. He may be coordinated enough to grab these biscuits on the first try. More likely, he will need to build up his timing skills before he consistently snags those treats.

Conclusion

Congratulations! You've become a master of clicker training and your dog has become one happy, obedient, trick-performing canine. Just like all good things in life, continue with the clicker training. Be imaginative and branch into other avenues.

Recognize that you are part of a fast-growing group of dog lovers who rely on the sound of a click to shape their dogs' behavior in a fun, positive way. To learn more, check out the great clicker resources on the following pages.

Helpful Web sites:

http://www.clickersolutions.com

ClickerSolutions is operated by Melissa Alexander, author of *Click for Joy!* The site provides information on clicker training, links to helpful sites, and ways to join a list service to share comments with others who engage in clicker training their dogs.

http://www.clickertraining.com

This comprehensive Web site is operated by Karen Pryor,

PhD, an animal behaviorist who is credited with popularizing the use of clicker training on dogs. Her site offers tips, resources, and instruction for hands-on training sessions.

Books:

Jones, Deborah, PhD. *Click & Go: Clicker Fun*. Colorado: Canine Training Systems, 1999.

Pryor, Karen. *Clicker Training Your Dog*. Massachusetts: Sunshine Books, Inc., 2001.

Tillman, Peggy. *Clicking With Your Dog: Step-by-Step in Pictures*. Massachusetts: Sunshine Books, Inc., 2001.

Pet expert **Arden Moore** is an award-winning author and professional speaker who specializes in writing about pets and on human health topics. She is a regular contributor to *Dog Fancy* and *Prevention* magazines as well as to the *Popular Dog* series. Moore belongs to the Dog Writers Association of America and the Association of Veterinary Communicators. She has authored numerous books, including *Healthy Dog: The Ultimate Fitness Guide for You and Your Dog*; *Dog Parties: How To Party With Your Pup*; *Dog Training: A Lifelong Guide*; *Happy Dog: How Busy People Care for Their Dogs*; *Tricks and Games*; *Real Food for Dogs*; and *50 Simple Ways to Pamper Your Dog*. She shares her Oceanside, California, home with her dog, Chipper, and three doglike cats, Murphy, Little Guy, and Callie. She can be reached through her Web site: http://www.byarden.com.

Buck Jones's humorous illustrations have appeared in numerous magazines (including *Dog Fancy* and *Cat Fancy*) and books. He is the illustrator for the best-selling Simple Solutions™ series, *Why Do Cockatiels Do That?*, *Why Do Parakeets Do That?*, *Kittens! Why Do They Do What They Do?*, and *Puppies! Why Do They Do What They Do?*